Happy Easter to ________________ .

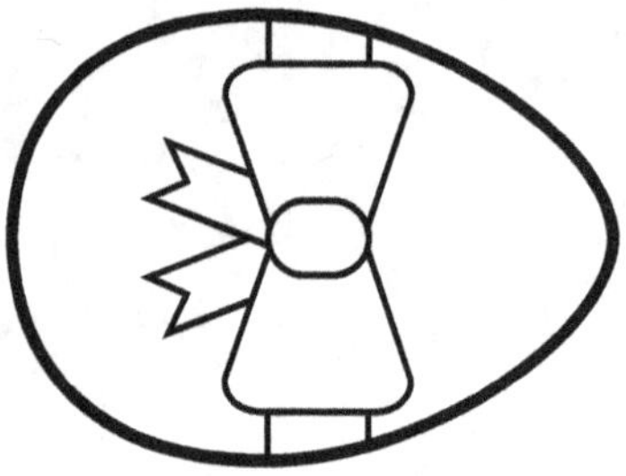

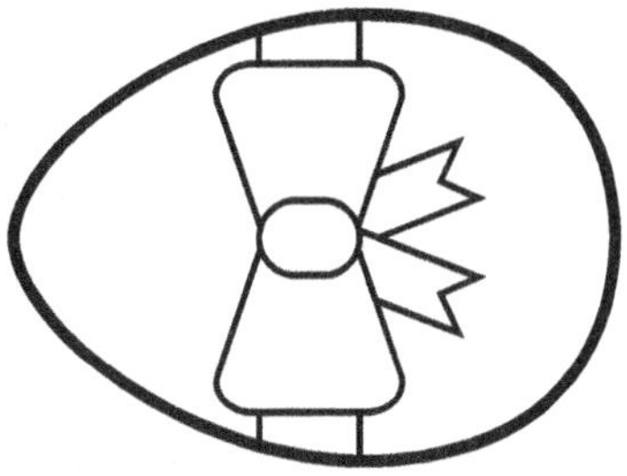

Mommy & Me Easter Coloring Book

Color With Me!

Sandy Mahony
Mary Lou Brown

HAPPY
EASTER

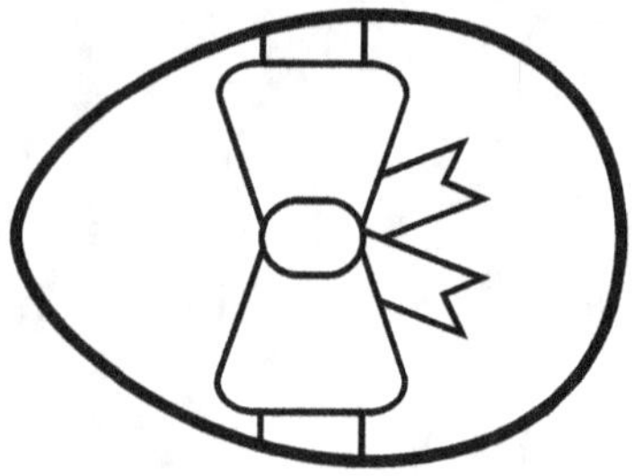

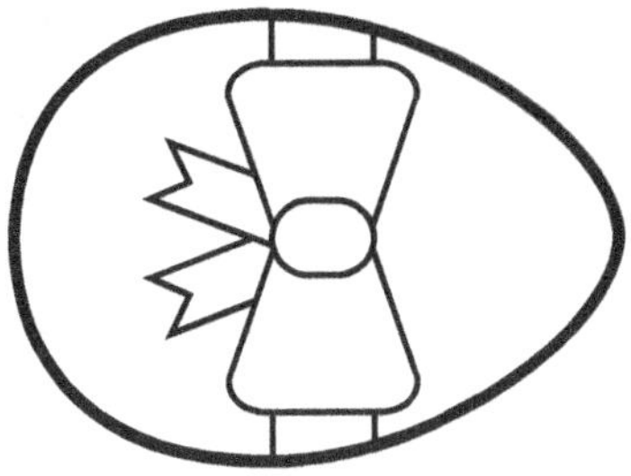
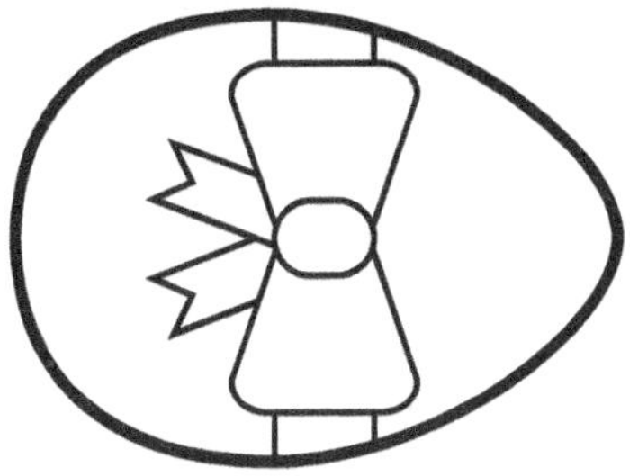
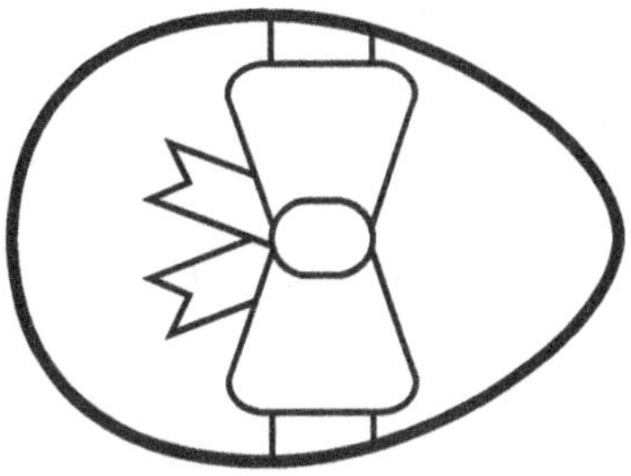
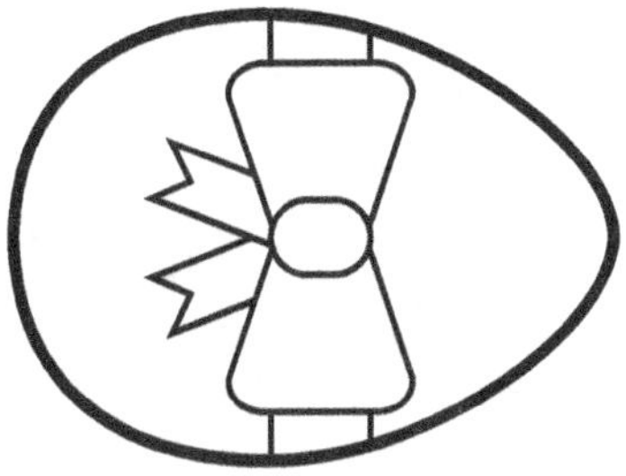

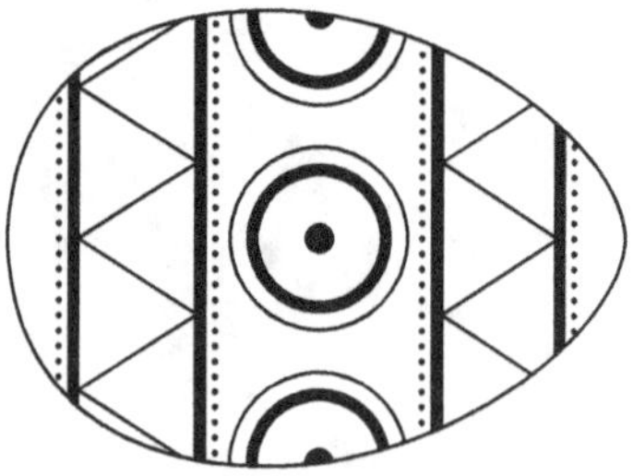
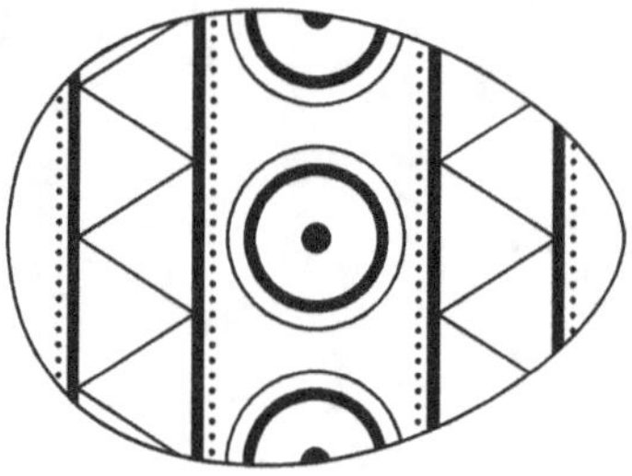
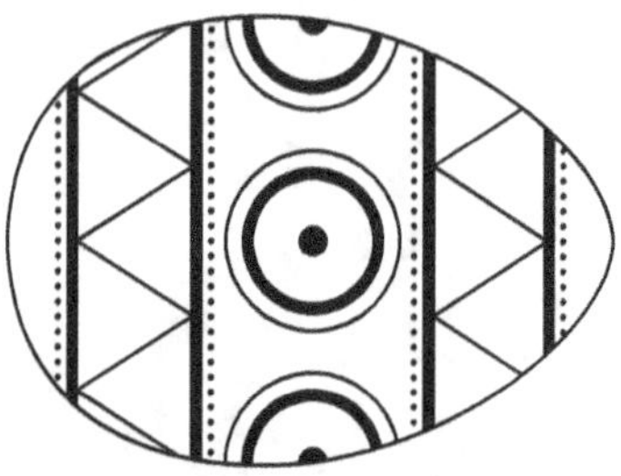
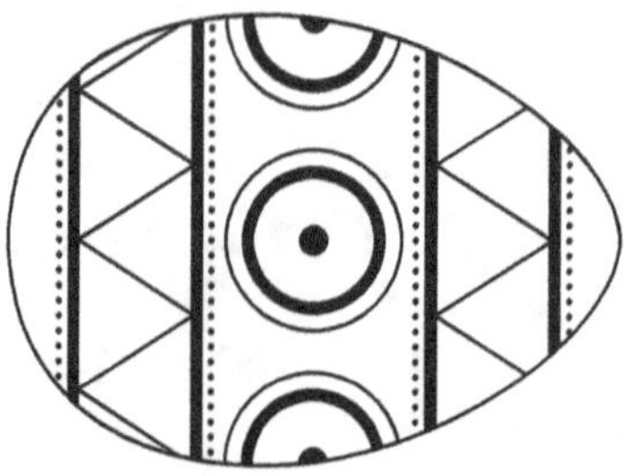

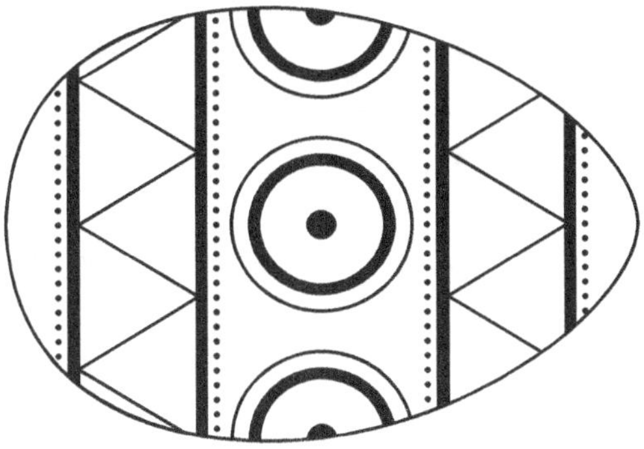
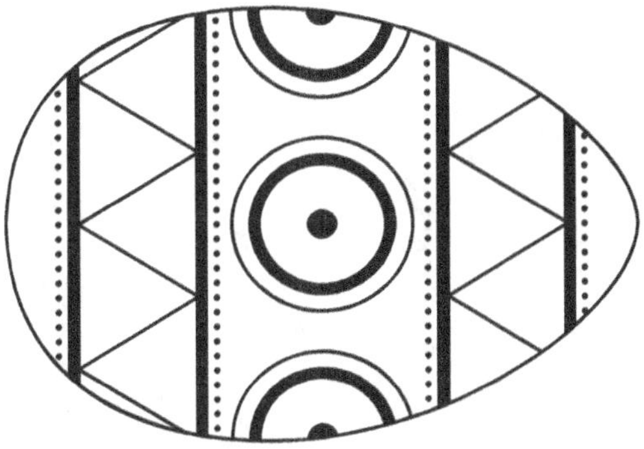

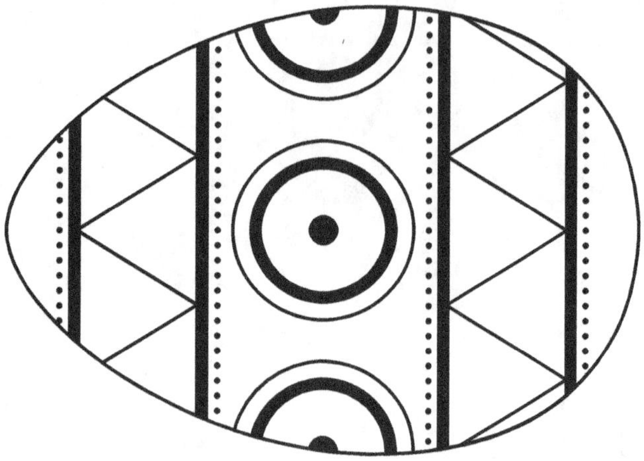

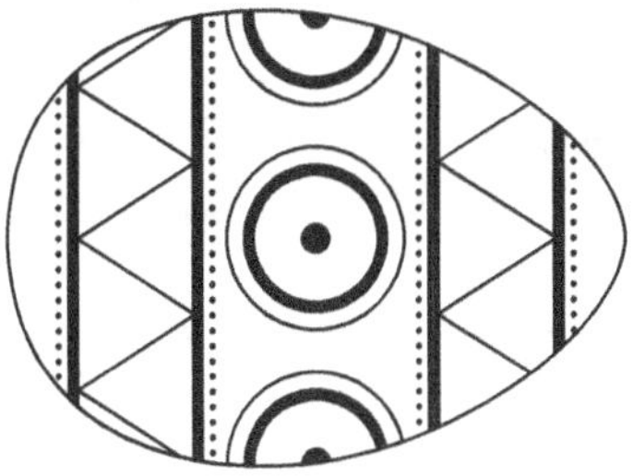
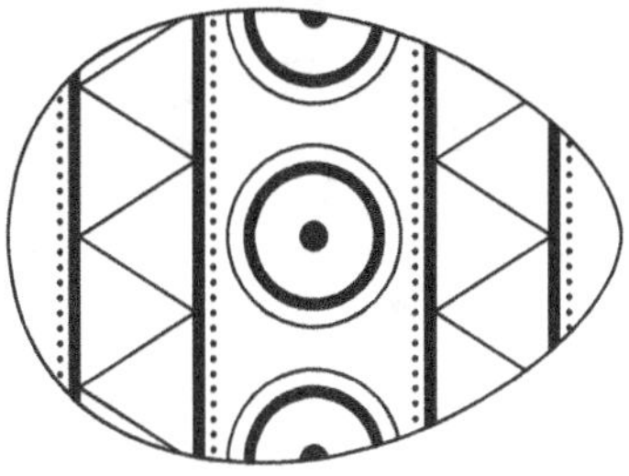
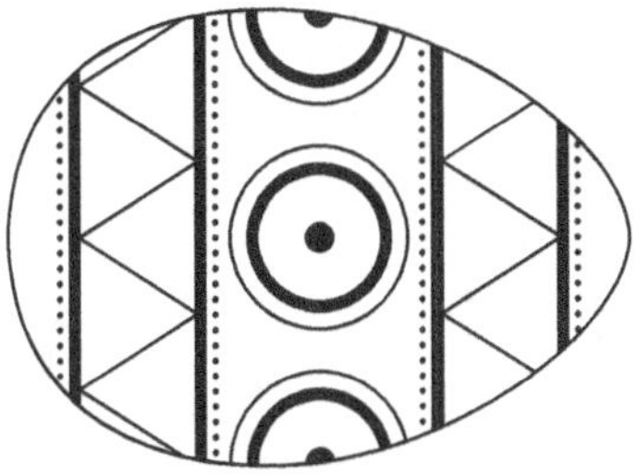
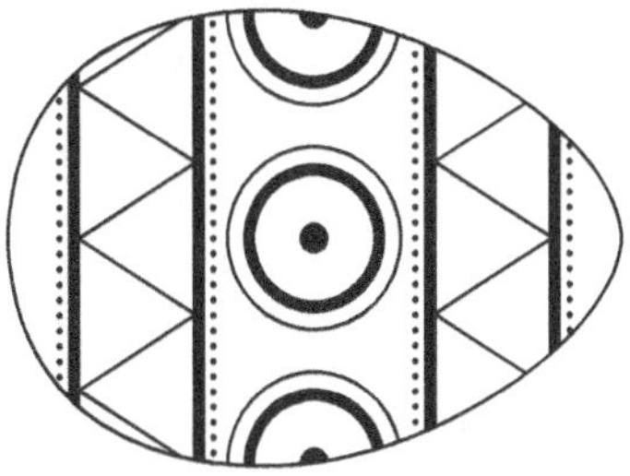

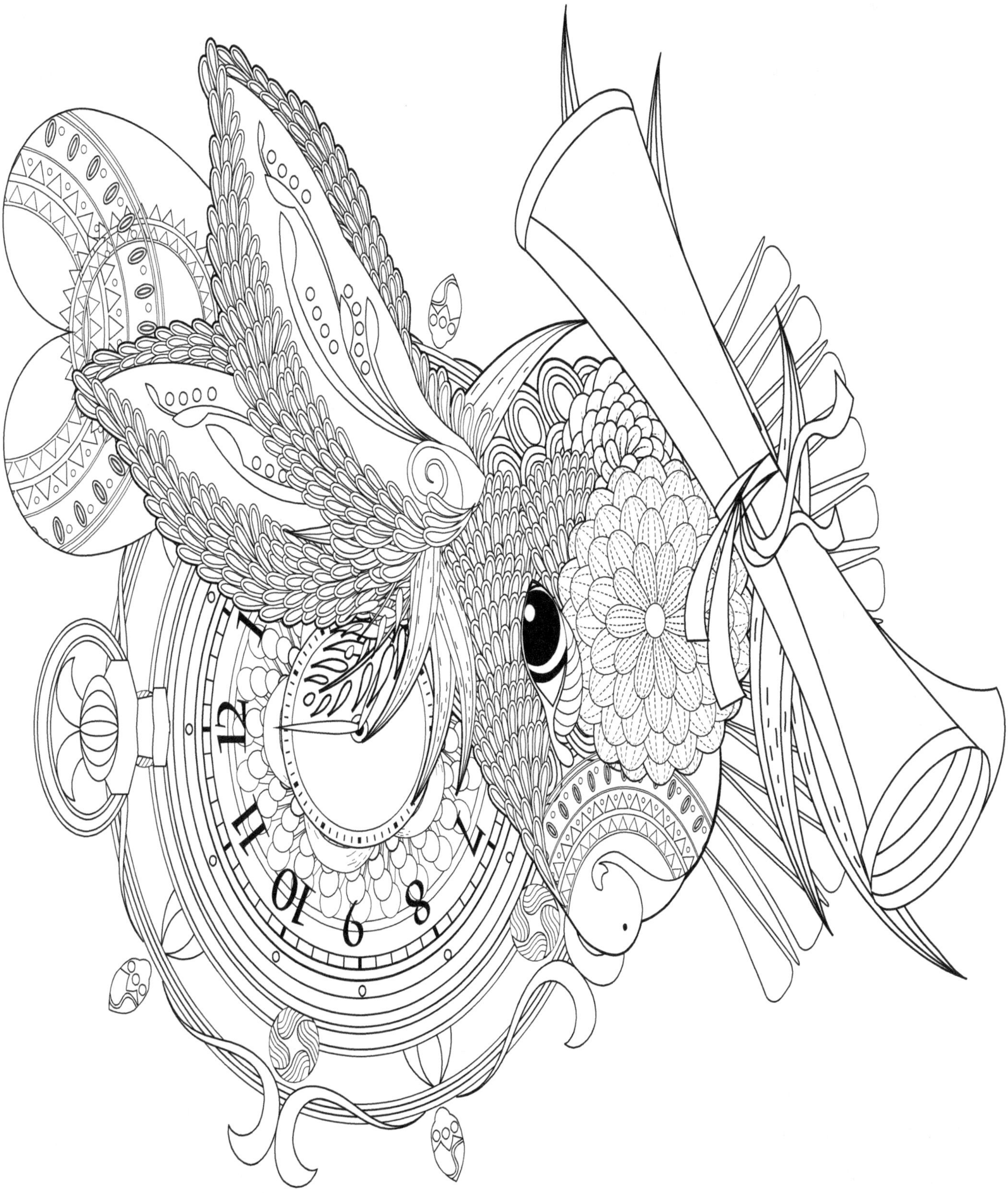

hello
Spring

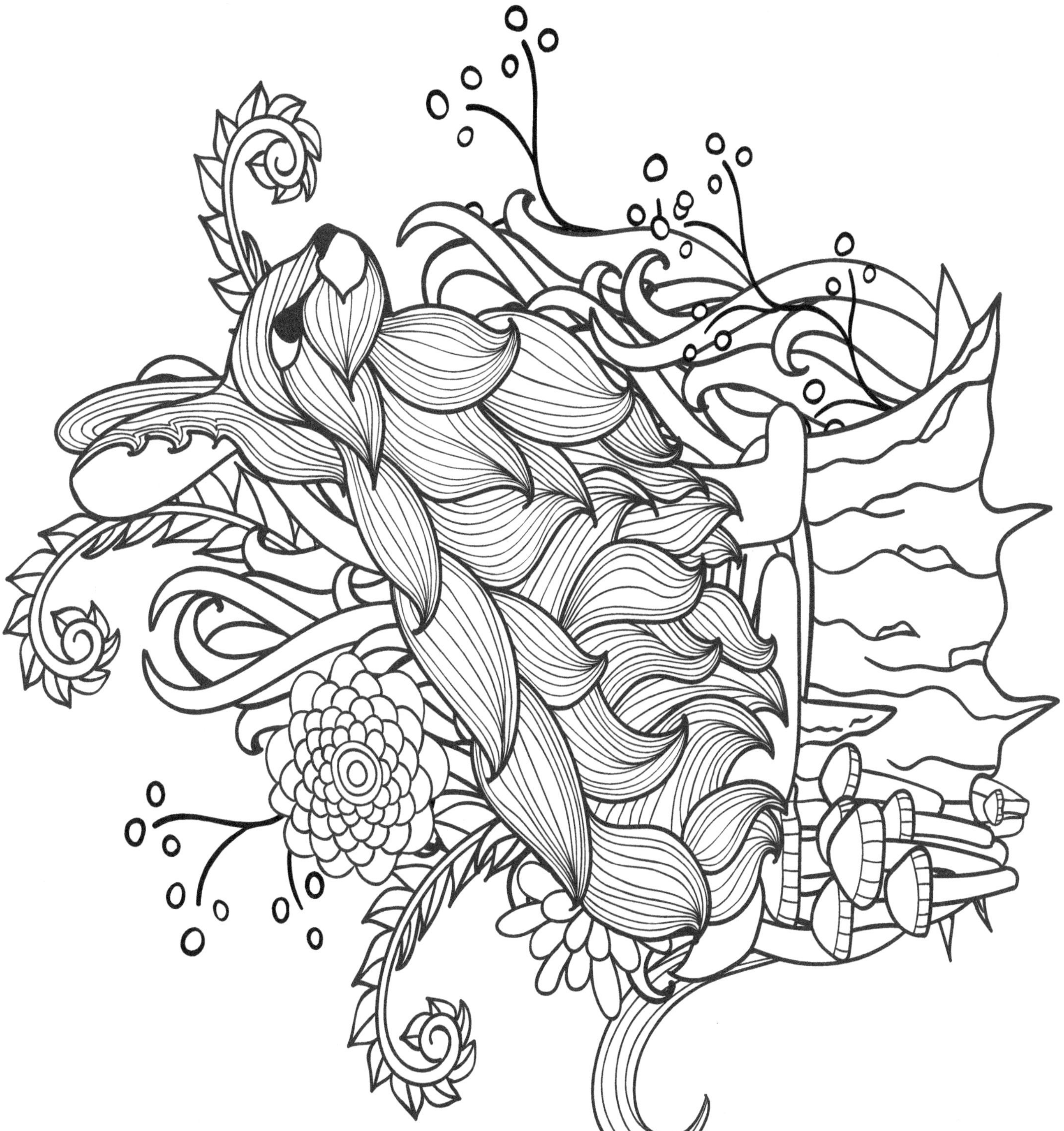

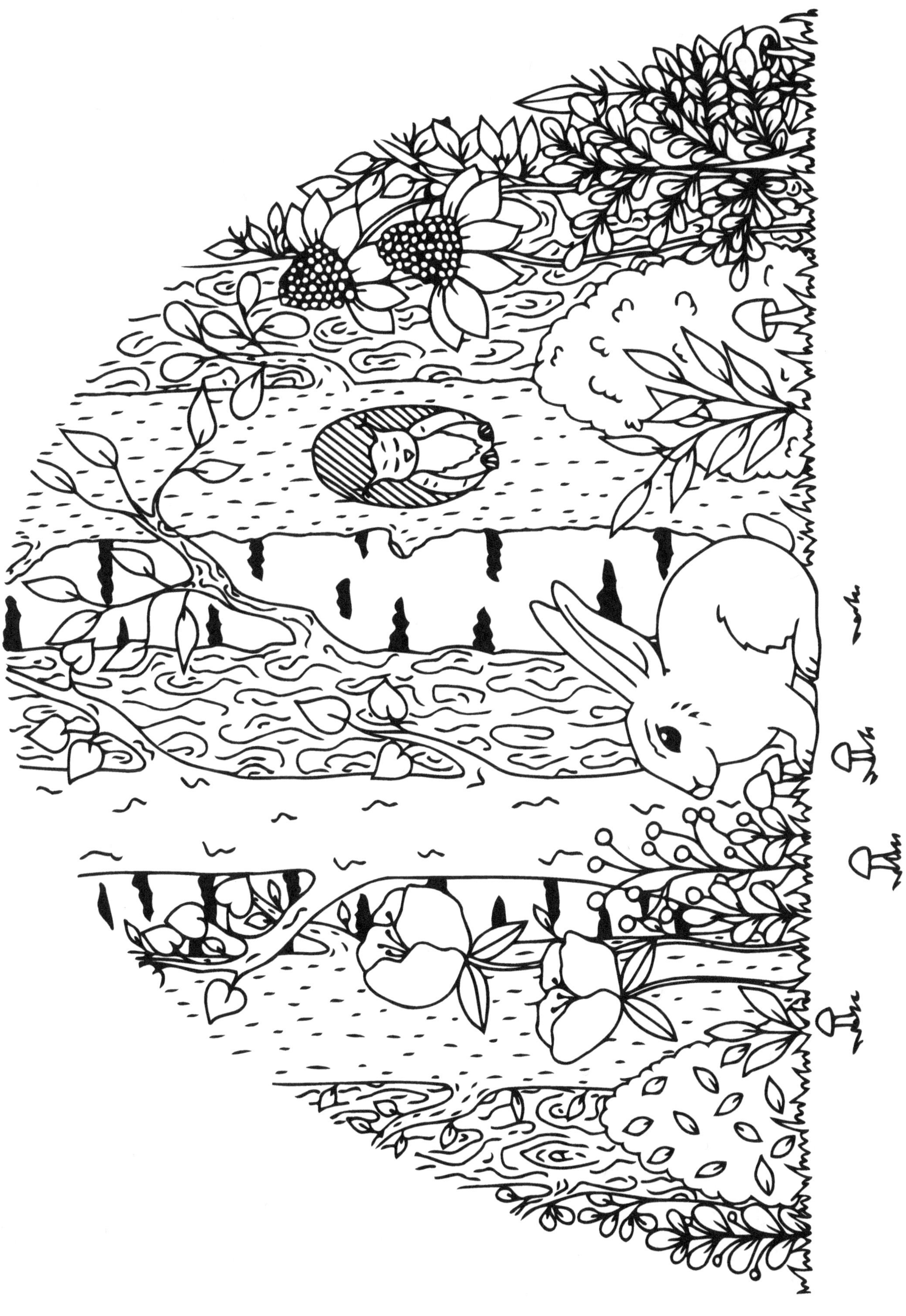

adventurelearningpress.com

www.ingramcontent.com/pod-product-compliance
Lightning Source LLC
Chambersburg PA
CBHW081411280526
45788CB00009B/3057
* 9 7 8 1 5 4 2 7 6 8 3 9 9 *